ANIMAL SAFARI

Wolverines

by Megan Borgert-Spaniol

BELLWETHER MEDIA • MINNEAPOLIS, MN

Note to Librarians, Teachers, and Parents:

Blastoff! Readers are carefully developed by literacy experts and combine standards-based content with developmentally appropriate text.

Level 1 provides the most support through repetition of high-frequency words, light text, predictable sentence patterns, and strong visual support.

Level 2 offers early readers a bit more challenge through varied simple sentences, increased text load, and less repetition of high-frequency words.

Level 3 advances early-fluent readers toward fluency through increased text and concept load, less reliance on visuals, longer sentences, and more literary language.

Level 4 builds reading stamina by providing more text per page, increased use of punctuation, greater variation in sentence patterns, and increasingly challenging vocabulary.

Level 5 encourages children to move from "learning to read" to "reading to learn" by providing even more text, varied writing styles, and less familiar topics.

Whichever book is right for your reader, Blastoff! Readers are the perfect books to build confidence and encourage a love of reading that will last a lifetime!

This edition first published in 2014 by Bellwether Media, Inc.

No part of this publication may be reproduced in whole or in part without written permission of the publisher. For information regarding permission, write to Bellwether Media, Inc., Attention: Permissions Department, 5357 Penn Avenue South, Minneapolis, MN 55419.

Library of Congress Cataloging-in-Publication Data

Borgert-Spaniol, Megan, 1989-
Wolverines / by Megan Borgert-Spaniol.
   p. cm. – (Blastoff! readers. Animal safari)
Summary: "Developed by literacy experts for students in kindergarten through grade three, this book introduces wolverines to young readers through leveled text and related photos"– Provided by publisher.
Audience: K to grade 3.
Includes bibliographical references and index.
ISBN 978-1-60014-916-0 (hardcover : alk. paper)
1. Wolverine–Juvenile literature. I. Title.
QL737.C25B6725 2014
599.76'6–dc23
                                                                      2013000890

Printed in the United States of America, North Mankato, MN.

Contents

What Are Wolverines?

Wolverines are strong **mammals**. They have **stocky** bodies.

Where Wolverines Live

Wolverines live in cold forests, mountains, and **plains**. Thick fur coats keep them warm.

Wide feet help wolverines run on top of deep snow.

They use their long, sharp **claws** to climb rocks and trees.

Hunting for Food

Wolverines often **scavenge**. Their strong **jaws** and teeth bite through **frozen** meat.

They sometimes wait for wolves or other animals to kill large **prey**. Then they chase these **predators** away.

Wolverines also hunt for rabbits, squirrels, and other small animals.

They run fast to catch their prey. They grab their meal by the neck.

Wolverines also hide in trees to wait for prey. Then they attack!

Glossary

claws–sharp, curved nails at the end of an animal's fingers and toes

frozen–made hard by the cold

jaws–the bones that form the mouth of an animal

mammals–warm-blooded animals that have backbones and feed their young milk

plains–large areas of flat land

predators–animals that hunt other animals for food

prey–animals that are hunted by other animals for food

scavenge–to feed on the meat of a dead animal

stocky–short and thick

To Learn More

AT THE LIBRARY

Markle, Sandra. *Wolverines*. Minneapolis, Minn.: Lerner Publications, 2005.

Markovics, Joyce L. *Wolverine: Super Strong*. New York, N.Y.: Bearport Pub., 2011.

Swanson, Diane. *Welcome to the World of Wolverines*. North Vancouver, B.C.: Whitecap Books, 2010.

ON THE WEB

Learning more about wolverines is as easy as 1, 2, 3.

1. Go to www.factsurfer.com.

2. Enter "wolverines" into the search box.

3. Click the "Surf" button and you will see a list of related Web sites.

With factsurfer.com, finding more information is just a click away.

Index

The images in this book are reproduced through the courtesy of: F1 Online/ SuperStock, front cover; Dieter Hopf/ Glow Images, p. 5; Minden Pictures/ SuperStock, p. 7; Brykaylo Yuriy, p. 7 (left); Pchais, p. 7 (middle); Ozerov Alexander, p. 7 (right); Robert Postma/ Glow Images, p. 9; K Salminen/ Age Fotostock, p. 11; Steven Kazlowski/ Getty Images, p. 13; Igor Shpilenok/ Nature Picture Library, p. 15; Age Fotostock/ SuperStock, p. 17; Alan Scheer, p. 17 (left); Nadiia Korol, p. 17 (right); NHPA/ SuperStock, p. 19; Juan Carlos Munoz/ Age Fotostock, p. 21.